OUT OF THE DUMP

WRITINGS AND PHOTOGRAPHS BY
CHILDREN FROM GUATEMALA

OUT OF THE DUMP

EDITED BY
KRISTINE L. FRANKLIN & NANCY McGIRR
TRANSLATED FROM THE SPANISH BY KRISTINE L. FRANKLIN

LOTHROP, LEE & SHEPARD BOOKS   NEW YORK

This book is dedicated to Rember Ramirez, who sparkled.
He will always live on in our hearts for his leadership,
his sense of fun, and his contagious enthusiasm.

Text copyright © 1995 by Kristine L. Franklin

Photographs copyright © 1995 by Out Of The Dump: Photographs by Children from Guatemala City's Garbage Dump

All rights reserved. No part of this book may be reproduced or utilized in any form or by any means, electronic or mechanical, including photocopying
and recording, or by any information storage and retrieval system, without permission in writing from the Publisher. Inquiries should be addressed to
Lothrop, Lee & Shepard Books, a division of William Morrow & Company, Inc., 1350 Avenue of the Americas, New York, New York 10019.

Printed in the United States of America

First Edition   1 2 3 4 5 6 7 8 9 10

Library of Congress Cataloging in Publication Data

Out of the dump: writings and photographs by children from Guatemala / edited by Kristine L. Franklin and Nancy McGirr.

p.   cm.

Summary: A compilation of poems with photographs by children who live in the municipal dump in Guatemala City.

ISBN 0-688-13923-X. — ISBN 0-688-13924-8 (lib. bdg.)

1. Children's writings, Guatemalan—Translations into English   2. Children's poetry, Guatemalan—Translations into English.
[1. Children's writings. 2. Guatemalan poetry—Collections.] I. Franklin, Kristine L. II. McGirr, Nancy.

PQ7496.5.E508 1995 861—dc20   95-9782 CIP AC

A NOTE ABOUT THIS BOOK

About 1,500 people, the majority of them children, live, eat, and work in the smoldering garbage dump in the center of Guatemala City. The dump is the end of the line for families that suffer severe poverty. They work hard—collecting cardboard, plastic, glass, and tin for recycling and scavanging for items to resell and food to eat. The children are expected to help, either by rooting through the refuse or by caring for their younger siblings while their parents work. In many cases, it is a financial hardship to spare an older child for school.

In 1991 I was photographing street children and trying to come up with a way to encourage them to get off the streets. I noticed their fascination with anything to do with my camera, and so came the idea of starting a project in which the kids would photograph their own world.

I brought a few cameras into the dump and let any child who wanted take pictures. Then I printed up small black-and-white prints of the portraits they took, and the children presented them to their subjects. This made us very popular in the dump and helped reinforce our acceptance in the community.

A photographer friend, Dennis Budd Gray, visited from Japan and took back some of the children's work to seek a sponsor for the project. Two months later, he called to say that Konica Japan wanted to help us. They generously supplied us with cameras, film, paper, batteries, et cetera. Eight children now had their own cameras, and we had our first exhibit scheduled for December 1992 in Tokyo.

DOUG FARAH
The Washington *Post*

A couple of months later, the children came to me and asked if I would put them in school. We had made some money selling notecards of their work, and that went for notebooks, pens, books, backpacks, and shoes. When they had been in school for several months, I made going to school a prerequisite for staying in the photography project.

The profits we now make from publications, notecards, prints, and exhibits go partly for educational expenses and for maintaining the project. The rest is divided evenly among the students. Because the children are contributing financially to their families, their parents can afford to spare them for school. The parents are an integral part of the project and participate enthusiastically.

"Out of the Dump" now has twenty-three children participating. Their work has been exhibited in London, Paris, Tokyo, Amsterdam, California, and Alabama, and the project has been featured on National Public Radio, Cable News Network, TV NHK Japan, and German public television, as well as in the Washington *Post* and the Los Angeles *Times*.

I feel very privileged to be working with such an extraordinary group of young photographers. Each of them began early to develop a personal style. They have learned to translate ideas into art, and their self-confidence and hope have grown alongside their skill with their cameras.

From the beginning, I've worked with the children not only to teach them photography and provide for their education, but to show them the power of dreaming. I tell them that photography is difficult and that if they can do this, they can do anything. There *are* options in life. For these children, photography has become a door to an exciting new world alive with possibilities. It is a door they have opened.

NANCY MCGIRR
Guatemala City, 1996

OUR ALLEY
by Marta Lopez

Three little houses
    guard our alley.
Three little houses
    full of children:
    five in my house,
        three behind,
        four across the alley.
We share the alley:
    it's where we play,
        where we walk,
        where we listen
        to people who fight.
We share the alley,
    but the clothesline?
    No!
My sister climbs a pole
    to hang the wet clothes.
    Later
    she stands guard
        so no one steals
        the clothes.
We share the alley,
    but the clothesline
        is ours.

Donna in our alley
MARTA LOPEZ

WHEN I'M A FATHER
by Rember Ramirez

When I'm a father I'll take good care of my old parents as long as they live. I'll take care of my children too, and work so they can eat. I'll take care of my children like my parents are taking care of me. I'll get them things they need, and I'll make sure they're educated.

I'm going to teach my children everything they need to know so they'll turn out to be good people. I won't allow them to hang around with bad people because bad people teach children things they didn't know before, like for example, how to sniff glue or how to smoke. I will never permit that.

I'm going to be a good father. I'll love and care for my children and teach them to read and write so they'll have a good future, just like my parents are doing for me now.

My father and brother read the Bible every afternoon
REMBER RAMIREZ

My stepfather taking a nap
JUNIOR RAMOS

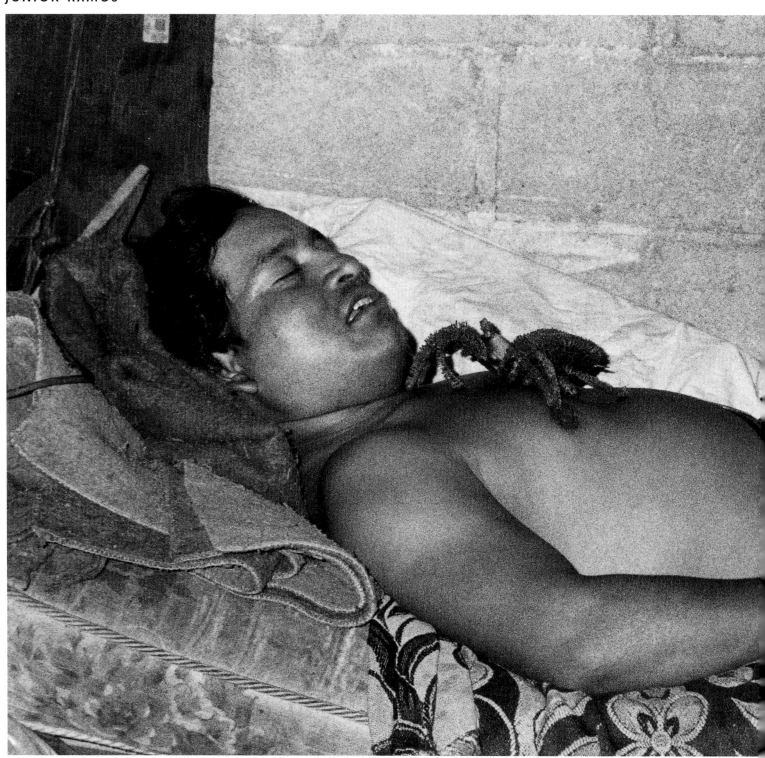

THE SPIDER
by Junior Ramos

The biggest spider
in the world.
I found it
in the house under my bed,
lurking in the shadows.

The biggest spider
in the world.
I found it,
a black one with spots,
hunting for food.

The biggest spider
in the world.
I caught it
and put it on my stepdad
sleeping on the bed.

The biggest spider
in the world.
I scared my mom.
My stepdad didn't wake up
even when she screamed.

The biggest spider
in the world.
My brother tore off
all of its legs and now
my rubber joke is dead.

My mother
ADELSO ORDOÑEZ

WHEN I'M A MOTHER
by Rosario Lopez

When I'm a mother, I'm going to educate my daughters. I'm going to teach them to do housework, like sweeping, washing the clothes, and cooking. I'm going to teach them how to buy everything they need to cook the important things like vegetables, chicken, rice, and beans.

When mothers don't educate their daughters it's bad because the daughters get sassy and then their mothers don't love them anymore. There are mothers who teach their daughters to smoke and give them everything they want. On the other hand, there are mothers who educate and care for their daughters.

Some girls don't want to lift a finger at home, and when they get married it will be horrible because they won't know a thing. A guy who marries a girl like that will soon be saying there are some women who only know how to fix themselves up and change their own clothes. An uneducated girl is worthless. Some mothers abandon their daughters because for them and for their husbands, a lazy girl is nothing but an annoyance.

My mother
GLADIZ JIMENEZ

The patio
ADELSO ORDOÑEZ

MORNING
by Marta Lopez

First
I hear my mother
waking me up.
I hear my little brothers
fighting on the floor.
I hear the sound of the dog
barking, begging for meat.
He cries with sadness
because there isn't any meat.
I would like meat too,
but I don't cry.
I eat beans
and my stomach
is happy.

BROTHERS AND SISTERS
by Gladiz Jimenez

Brothers and sisters
should love each other.
They're from the same family,
of the same mother,
of the same blood.
They shouldn't fight.
Mother is ready,
with a belt in her hand,
to see who fights
and who doesn't,
for hate is a sin.
Brothers and sisters should
love each other,
like and
respect one another,
so there can be
love and peace on earth.
If there is peace in the home
there is love in the world.

My little brother and sister
GLADIZ JIMENEZ

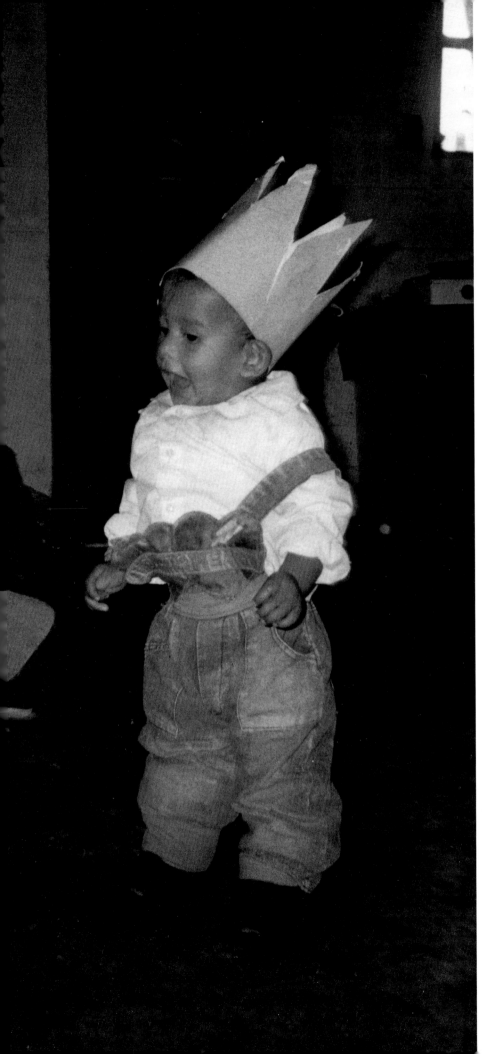

KING OF THE HOUSE
by Gladiz Jimenez

My little brother,
a two-year old baby,
is the biggest person
in the family.
No one can smack him
because if they do,
my mother defends him.
He gets more food,
more money,
more clothes and shoes.
He eats more meat.
He always gets the best.
When my father comes home
the baby yells,
"Daddy!"
When he sees his little son
my father says,
"My son!"
The baby
is the king.

My little brother
BENITO SANTOS

Rosario in her house
BENITO SANTOS

TAKING PICTURES
by Junior Ramos

In the photography class they taught me to take pictures. First I learned to put the film in the camera. Then I learned that the most important things to remember are the angle and the lighting. After that, I learned to take photographs.

I like taking pictures of parties best, because at a party everyone is dancing. Watching people dance makes me want to dance too. The music is always happy, with a rock beat. When I take a picture of the sound equipment, I am taking a picture of the music itself. That way I can remember the party forever. I want to take pictures for the rest of my life.

Watching the feast-day procession in Solala
JUNIOR RAMOS

PLANE CRASH
by Rember Ramirez

I was visiting a neighbor lady and we were watching the news on TV. All of a sudden they were showing a TACA plane that had crashed in a little town. I took a photo of the crash just to see how it would turn out.

No one died in that crash. The neighbor lady told us it was because she had ten pictures of Mary and Jesus and four statues of Jesus in her house. She burns candles to the pictures and statues and gives them flowers, and they protect her from evil. She's a very good Catholic and has ten children. She's a witch too, and she can take evil spirits out of people and remove curses with candles, lemons, eggs, a handful of seven herbs, alcohol, and the ashes from incense.

The night the TACA flight crashed
REMBER RAMIREZ

Don Celso washes plastic bags to resell
REMBER RAMIREZ

THE BAG MAN
by **Rember Ramirez**

Don Celso looks for bags
 to wash, to sell, to buy clothes
  for his four kids.
Bags of every size,
 bags and bags,
  plastic bags,
   and sheets of plastic too.
If he could only find something electric.
 What luck!
  A lamp or an iron,
  would be a treasure
   to him.

OLD WOMAN
by Gladiz Jimenez

The oldest woman
at the dump dresses
in a tattered Indian skirt.
Her clothes are torn,
she goes barefoot all the time,
her face is very wrinkled.
Even her eyelids are wrinkled.
They cover up
her old brown eyes.
It is a sad face
because she's depressed.
Her daughter died.
The old woman used to sell gum
and fruit drinks on the street,
but now she doesn't do a thing.
She used to live
with her thirteen-year old granddaughter,
but the granddaughter got married.
Now she lives alone,
the poor old sad woman.

Oldest Woman
GLADIZ JIMENEZ

Her fifteenth birthday
MIRIAN ESQUIVEL

FIFTEENTH BIRTHDAY
by Rosario Lopez

When a girl turns fifteen, it's a happy time. Her parents give her a cake, candies, balloons, a piñata, and other things she has asked them to buy. Most girls want shoes, dresses, and earrings, but their parents always say that they can't spend that much money. Since all of a girl's sisters will also have a fifteenth birthday someday, she can't have everything she asks for. She has to choose what she wants most and it has to be something useful, like clothes or shoes. She's not supposed to ask for something expensive, like a bicycle, because there is never enough money for things like that. And besides, when a girl is twenty years old, she doesn't use a bicycle anymore. If parents bought everything their birthday girl wanted, they'd be left without a cent.

WOMEN AND THEIR CHILDREN
by Mirian Esquivel

Women always have a lot of children because they fall in love when they're only fifteen years old. When they're sixteen they start to have babies. Since men want other women, they leave the ones with children and go off with new women, so the women have two children by one man, maybe three by another, or maybe just one or two. If the men stayed with their families, they wouldn't work anyway, and the women would have to work harder.

I know a woman with ten children. Her husband left her, so she put a curse on him. He died from the curse. Now that woman lives happily with her ten children.

The Anonymous Couple
REMBER RAMIREZ

The Jar
GLADIZ JIMENEZ

THE JAR
by Gladiz Jimenez

I don't ever want to get married because having a husband is nothing but a big problem. Husbands beat up their children and yell a lot and throw things and drink, and when they're drinking they don't work.

My father drinks. He used to drink a lot more; in fact, he was drinking so much we all thought he would die. Then my mother found a jar buried behind our house. Inside the jar was a photograph of my father and written on the back it said "DIE." Someone had put a curse on my father to make him die. My mother ripped up the photo and broke the jar and now my father hardly ever gets drunk.

We don't know who wanted to kill my father. If my mother hadn't found that jar, he would be dead by now.

*My brother crying because
my parents are fighting*
ADELSO ORDOÑEZ

*My sister among the
clothes my father threw
when he was drunk*
ADELSO ORDOÑEZ

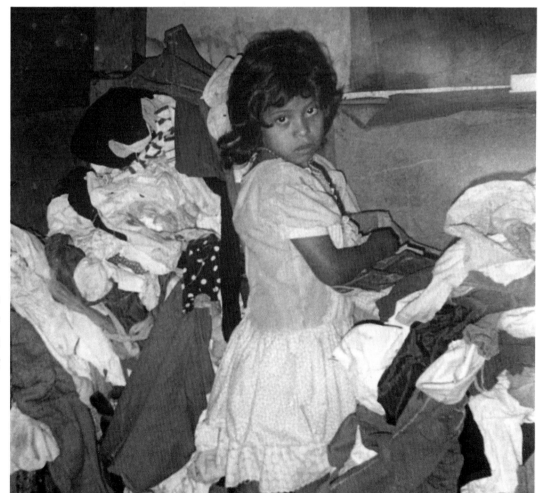

The atole vender
REMBER RAMIREZ

ATOLE
by Junior Ramos

Atole is
a magic vitamin.
It gives me energy.
It makes me strong.
It's sweet and hot,
made with
bananas,
milk,
and rice.
Made with
oatmeal,
or cornmeal,
or beanmeal,
it only costs
1 quetzal
at the store
or on the street.

SMELLS
by Marta Lopez

In my house
there are many smells:
smoke from the fire,
the boiling beans,
and always
tortillas
fresh and hot.
My stomach
shouts with hunger
when I smell
the delicious
tortillas.

Mother making tortillas
ROSARIO LOPEZ

THINGS PEOPLE FIND IN THE GARBAGE

by Marta Lopez

People find many things in the dump. They find shoes, clothing, gold and silver, dresses, earrings, rings, bracelets, dead bodies, and strangled children. One day a neighbor lady found a strangled girl in a box and when the tractor scooped up the box it made the lady

so sad that she put the little girl where the tractor couldn't get her again.

One day another lady found a big pig in the dump. The people surrounded it and she went to look for her sons. When the lady and her sons arrived, the people had left and the vultures were already eating the pig. The lady was so sad she ran away crying because she thought that the people had attacked and killed the pig.

Another day, a lady was collecting cardboard. Under the pile of cardboard she found a dead man. She called the police, but of course they couldn't figure anything out, except that whoever killed the man either ran away or was hiding somewhere.

The day we found the dead body in the dump
MIRIAN ESQUIVEL

LIKE A PRINCESS
by Rosario Lopez

Sometimes I find treasures
in the trash.
I like the toys,
the dolls and the balls,
but toys are for six-year-olds
and now I'm eleven.
I'd like something new.
Now I'd like to find
a purple silk skirt,
flat, black shoes,
the kind that shine
like a mirror,
a pink silk blouse
with long sleeves, with lace.
I'd like to find a gold necklace,
and a golden bracelet too,
and a ring with a diamond
that gives light like a star,
and dressed this way
I would walk around
as happy as a princess.

Self-portrait as a Spanish dancer
MIRIAN ESQUIVEL

**Barbies on a blanket
(scavenged from the dump)**
MIRIAN ESQUIVEL

MY FAVORITE FRIEND
by Rosario Lopez

Dolores is my favorite friend. We play and talk together during recess, and we help each other when the boys tease Dolores for being fat. One day the boys called her funny nicknames and we all laughed. When Dolores figured out that we were laughing at her, we had to hide from her because she threw mango pits at us. She hit some of the kids and they started to cry.

After recess those kids complained to the teacher and he called Dolores up and asked her what was going on. She said everyone was calling her names, and he wanted to know what names. She told him the kids were calling her "elephant" and "hippopotamus," and the teacher laughed too. Dolores started to cry, and when she got home she told her mother everything.

Dolores's mother came to school and complained. The teacher told her that her daughter Dolores was now a famous joke, so famous, in fact, that he was thinking of sending her name to all the newspapers in every county. The lady got really furious and told the teacher he was a rude, filthy pig for teaching his students to make fun of others.

Visiting my cousin
BENITO SANTOS

THE CHINAMAN
by Rember Ramirez

The Chinaman,
that's him.
The Chinaman.
For all we know
he doesn't have
another name.
He's kind, a joker.
He gives goodies
to the children,
and clothes
and sometimes toys.
He's lived at the dump
for fifteen years
and never
wants to leave.
He buys
and sells
old sheet metal.
Buys for 5.
Sells for 20.
He says he's not rich,
but I think he is.
He carries his money
in a secret pocket.

El Chino, the scrap dealer
BENITO SANTOS

The cat
ADELSO ORDOÑEZ

THE CAT
by Marta Lopez

When my grandmother was young she had a new baby. She noticed that the cat was always watching the baby and she worried about it so much she couldn't sleep. Day and night she stayed awake, but one evening she was so sleepy she fell asleep. In the night, the cat stole the baby.

At dawn my grandmother awoke and of course the baby was not in bed with her, so she called her other children to come help look for it. When they found the baby it was under the bed, completely green and stiff and dead.

OLD FOLKS
by Rember Ramirez

Old folks

go

to the dump

when

they can't work to

look for

things to sell

so

they can buy bread.

So old!

They have

no strength

to work.

Walk so slow.

It's hard to eat

because

they have no teeth.

They sleep

in the street

under

cardboard roofs.

A portrait of my grandmother
JUNIOR RAMOS

Boys jumping on a trampoline made from old mattress springs and cardboard
BENITO SANTOS
& RONY VASQUEZ

Coming home from school
MARTA LOPEZ

BOYS
by Rosario Lopez

All boys want to do is play, watch television, bother everyone, talk back, and sleep all night long until it's time to eat again. They want to go to school to play with their friends and to bug the girls.

All the boys in my class think about is going to the cemetery, even though it's not allowed. One day our teacher didn't show up and we girls stayed to play in the classroom while the boys left. When they got back, the principal asked us if it was true that everyone had gone to the cemetery. We said no, we didn't go, but he hit us with a ruler anyway. The next day the teacher came back, and wanted to know if we'd behaved well or not. After she talked to the principal she bawled us out. We all sat down, but the boys started acting up, saying they were going back to the cemetery. When it was recess, they left. When they came back, the teacher was waiting at the door. She hit them all with the ruler and every day from then on they had to stand up in class and if she even noticed them, she hit them again.

THE BEST PET
by Junior Ramos

My dog is the best pet in the world. He plays with me, loves me, and takes care of me when I go to the store or some other place far from home. We play together on the patio at my house. Sometimes we go out and run in the street, and if another dog wants to bite me, my dog defends me. I love him like I love my family because he is good to me. With other people he isn't so great, especially if they are strangers. He only minds family members.

My dog sleeps in a little wooden house that I built and painted for him. He likes it a lot. Every morning I give him water and bones to eat and he finishes them quickly. I love my dog a lot. That's why I won't sell him or give him away, and I don't hit him—well, sometimes if he doesn't mind I hit him, but never hard, and I don't hurt him. Sometimes I take him for walks.

The ball
ADELSO ORDOÑEZ

Dog biting a stocking
GLADIZ JIMENEZ

DOGS
by Junior Ramos

Dump dogs
   are ferocious,
      biting,
      running,
      barking.
They stink
   like dead things.
They eat cats,
   rats,
   little mice too.

They fight over bones
     that they find in the trash.
They're fat from eating
    everything they see.
Dogs scare me.
   They go around
   searching for food
     and maybe,
     just maybe,
     I'll be
     the next meal.

READING LESSON
by Gladiz Jimenez

Our teacher teaches us the vowels.
If we don't learn them
she repeats
A E I O U
until we have them memorized
frontwards and backwards.
The lesson called "mama"
goes like this:
ma me mi mo mu.
"Repeat it," says the teacher,
and we do, and then
we learn to write Mama,
the most important word.
I want to read it all,
stories, books,
signs in the street,
the menu in a restaurant.
But before I read
I must review
ma me mi mo mu.
My parents can't read.
They can only write
their names.
Maybe I
will be their teacher.
Ma me mi mo mu.

My mother
ADELSO ORDOÑEZ

MIRROR MIRROR
by Mirian Esquivel

The mirror is bewitched.
At night in the dark,
looking in the mirror,
I can see the shadow
of an evil spirit.
I sleep a while,
but the crickets
make a lot of noise
and I know an evil spirit
walks round
and round
my house.
Looking in the mirror
I'm scared to death,
so every night
Mama covers it up.
That way
nothing bad
can happen
to me.

A friend of my father
ROSARIO LOPEZ

THE EVIL EYE
by Rosario Lopez

The evil eye is a sickness that drunk men give to babies when they look at them. It happens by accident. Drunks have very strong eyes. The evil eye is cured with an egg, liquor, and seven herbs. Those who drink have to help cure the evil eye. They have to buy whatever is necessary for the cure.

Sometimes the evil eye is very strong. Then the drunks have to go with the parents and the sick babies to the doctor. They have to do whatever the doctor tells them. They have to get down on their knees. They have to ask the forgiveness of the parents for the evil they have done. Afterwards, they have to go to the graves of their own mothers and ask them for forgiveness too. By witchcraft, the mothers answer from the grave, and the babies are cured of the evil eye.

The Evil Eye
EDGAR VALENZUELA

My aunts in the highlands
MARTA LOPEZ

THE TWINS
by Marta Lopez

One day my aunt had twins. They were so sick from the evil eye that she had to take them to the doctor, but the doctor didn't cure them. With another woman, my aunt went to the Quiche region. They took the twins to see a woman who can cure the evil eye. My aunt asked her, "Why do my twins get sick so much?" The *curandera* answered, "It's because your husband beats up your older son." How it hurt my poor aunt to know that her twins were sick because of what her husband had done!

THE PRISONER
by Marta Lopez

It's possible this girl is a beautiful princess and a witch put a spell on her and now she's trapped in a poor house of tin and boards next to the garbage dump. Soon her soldiers and her prince will rescue her. She will escape! Her magicians will find that witch and put an end to her evil tricks. Then the princess will throw off her rags. She'll put on an elegant gown. She'll put on wooden shoes that never wear out, and leave forever with her prince. They'll fly to another world, to the United States, or even better, to Holland.

A little girl in her house
MARTA LOPEZ

WE DANCE
by Mirian Esquivel

Dance,
                dance.
        We love to move,
    to show off our bodies,
        to sway
                like wildcats,
                    to toss ourselves
        from side to side.
                Dance,
                    we dance.
            It's like we have
                    a spirit inside
        that fills us with joy,
    that makes us laugh.
                We dance
                    we dance
                        as though
                the music
            were
    bewitched.

Dancing
ROSARIO LOPEZ

MY COUNTRY
by Rember Ramirez

My country is a great place. It's big, and there are many good people. My country has bad people too, and there are problems. Among us poor people there is violence, killing, and assaults. What we need is money, and money is just an illusion.

Guatemala would be a better place if all the people would work together in order to live in peace, to end the violence. But the way it is with us, we know we could die any day, any hour. Our country is beautiful, lovely. It's a shame Guatemala is destroying itself.

My Country
EVELYN MANSILLA

A river near the seacoast
GUSTAVO HERNANDEZ